W9-DJL-020

LIFTING OREGON OUT OF THE MUD

Building the Oregon Coast Highway

You must wake and call me early
Call me early, Mother dear,
For soon will come the greatest day
That we will see this year.
T'will be the gayest day, Mother,
The jolliest, happiest day,
For we're dedicating our new bridge
That crosses the Alsea Bay.

—Clara M. Cooper

For dedication of Alsea Bay Bridge, *Waldport Tribune*, May 7, 1936

Joe R. Blakely

Other books by Joe Blakely

A Tribute to McArthur Court, 1891-1932

The Bellfountain Giant Killers
A miraculous 1937 state high school basketball championship

Eugene's Civic Stadium
From muddy football games to professional baseball

The Tall Firs
1939: The First NCAA Basketball Champions

NOVELS

Kidnapped
On Oregon's Coast Highway (1926)

The Heirloom
Bandon, Oregon (1921)

LIFTING OREGON OUT OF THE MUD
Building the Oregon Coast Highway

Joe R. Blakely

Author of *The Bellfountain Giant Killers* and *The Tall Firs*

CraneDance Publications
Eugene, OR

Lifting Oregon Out of the Mud
Building the Oregon Coast Highway

Copyright © 2006 by Joe R. Blakely

All rights reserved.

CraneDance Publications

HISTORICAL PHOTOGRAPHS

Photographs of the Roosevelt Highway and its bridges are reprinted with permission of the Oregon Department of Transportation History Center, Salem, Oregon. Other historical photographs were provided by Bear Creek Press archives, the Coos County Historical Museum, and Lorraine Eckhardt.

CONTEMPORARY PHOTOGRAPHS BY
Joe R. Blakely of Eugene, Oregon

PUBLISHED BY CRANEDANCE PUBLICATIONS
PO Box 50535, Eugene OR 97405
(541) 345-3974 • www.cranedance.com
April 2010
ISBN: 978-0-9824441-4-6

Printed in the United States of America

PRINTING HISTORY
Bear Creek Press First edition: April 2006,
under ISBN: 1-930111-60-6
Expanded: March 2008
Third printing: August 2009

I dedicate this book to my son, Justin R. Blakely,
who is my inspiration.

Get Oregon Out of the Mud.

—1913 slogan of the Oregon State Highway Commission
predecessor to the Oregon Department of Transportation

Acknowledgments

I am indebted to the following: Special thanks to Patricia A. Solomon (archivist), Laura E. Wilt (librarian), and Chris Leedham (structural design engineer) of the Oregon Department of Transportation, for their time, labor, and generosity in finding and sharing historical photographs of the Roosevelt Highway, and to my publishers, initially Bear Creek Press and now CraneDance Publications.

I would also like to thank Jodi Weeber of the Oregon Coast History Center and Liisa Penner of the Clatsop County Historical Society, who did their very best, even better than their very best, answering my many questions about the Roosevelt Highway.

Thanks also to the helpful people at the Coos County Historical Museum, the Lane County Historical Museum, the Curry County Historical Museum, the Historic Alsea Bay Bridge Interpretive Center, the University of Oregon Library (especially the microfilm department), the Oregon State Library and Archives, and the Eugene Public Library. Thanks also to Lorraine Eckhardt, who thoughtfully provided many old family photographs of the area around Tillamook, Oregon.

And thanks, also, to Saundra Miles for editing, to Karen Higgins for donating a copy of the 1964 *Curry County Reporter Golden Jubilee Edition*, and to John Heffley for lending me his 1920 *Automobile Blue Book*.

Contents

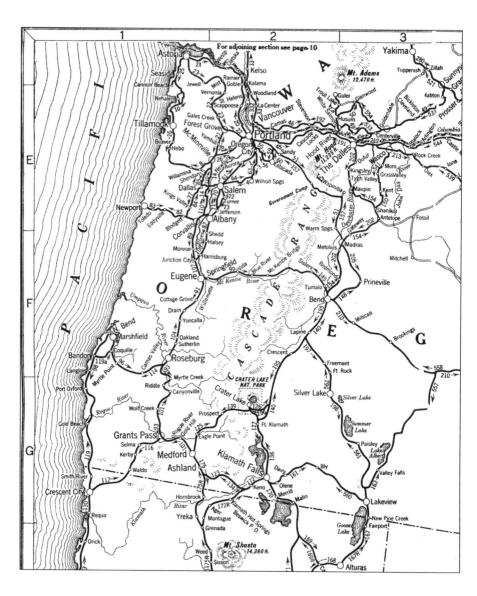

Oregon Road Map
1920

Battling Mud
1913-1918

In January of 1918, when Oregon auto dealer George A. Laffaw drove the 161 miles from Coos Bay—then called Marshfield—south to Crescent City, California to supervise the delivery of a shipment of Maxwell cars, he learned the hard way about the condition of roads along Oregon's coast. Accompanied by his mechanic and driving only during daylight hours, Laffaw left Coos Bay on a Monday afternoon and arrived in Crescent City on Wednesday, fifty-one hours later. "The roads were almost beyond description," the *Coos Bay Times* reported about the journey, "and the party had a merry time negotiating the many mud holes along the route."

The return trip, however, was even worse. Laffaw and his mechanic went through seven tires and three sets of chains, found the route to be "a sea of mud" at times reaching "6 inches over their running boards," and barely found enough time to eat. At Gold Beach, the Rogue River was so high that the ferryman refused to take them across until the following morning. Once across, it took more than five hours to travel sixteen miles to Corbin. "One of the most remarkable journeys ever made in this section of Oregon," the *Coos Bay Times* reported when the pair finally returned.

Along the Oregon coast, roads—or a lack of them—have been a big problem with a long history. As late as the early twentieth century, the roads on the northern coast were few and primi-

Motorist digging out his car on the central Oregon coast, 1912

tive, restricted mostly to a route between Tillamook and Astoria;
the central coast had almost no roads at all, though one did exist
inland between Newport and Corvallis (today's Highway 20);
and the southern coast had one primitive road from the interior—
the Coos Bay Wagon Road, which linked the Coos Bay area with
Roseburg. At the same time, however, newspapers everywhere
had begun passing the word about a new revolution in transportation—the automobile.

The first sale of an American gas car, a Daimler, occurred in
1896; the Model T Ford or "Tin Lizzie" was introduced in 1908.
When such cars as well as other models met with instant popular-
ity, their increased demand and production made it evident that
the state needed better roads—especially along the coast. Con-
fronting this problem became the job of the Oregon State Highway Commission, created in 1913.

The first commission consisted of three top state officials:
Treasurer Thomas Kay, Secretary of State Ben Olcott, and Gov-

ernor Oswald West. More than anyone else, it was West who was responsible for establishing the entire Oregon beach as a public highway, introducing the bill to the 1913 state legislature.

"I pointed out that thus we would come into miles and miles of highway without cost to the taxpayer," he wrote. "The legislature took the bait—hook, line and sinker. Thus came public ownership of our beaches."

Oswald West

At the time, the state's beaches were used extensively not only by horse-drawn buggies and stages—with wide rims making it easier to negotiate the soft sand—but also by growing numbers of automobiles because these were the only connections between some coastal towns. (This was true even after the arrival of the Southern Pacific Railroad to the area in 1916.) In spite of quick sand, river crossings, and sneaker waves along these routes, it was common to see beaches filled with so many people and cars that it resembled a modern-day parking lot.

On the southern Oregon coast, the Coos Bay Stage stops along its beach route.

Horse and buggy rescues stranded motorist along the Oregon coast

The year following the beach law, the commission adopted a report of Major Henry L. Bowlby, Oregon's first state highway engineer, who laid out a proposed network of five major state highways: the Pacific Highway (today's Interstate 5, which roughly follows part of the old Oregon Trail's Southern Route); The Dalles-California Highway (today's Highway 97); the Columbia River Highway (today's Columbia River Gorge Historic Highway, which was replaced as a major thoroughfare first with Highway 30 and then with Interstate 84); an "East-West" highway from Eugene, along the McKenzie River and over the Cascades (today's Highway 126, which follows part of the old Oregon Trail's Free Emigrant Road); and the Oregon Beach Highway (today's Highway 101 within Oregon). The highway along the coast was also to have two "loops" that connected to the inland before circling back to the beach, one in the north and another in the south.

Even though the beginning of World War I that year initially turned attention away from this highway system, an interim Oregon Legislative Assembly in 1917 shifted road-building responsibilities from the counties to the state, and it requested that the redesigned Oregon Highway Commission undertake "to enlarge the state highway system to 4,317 miles."

4

Financing for the system would be provided through a $6 million bond issued by the state, and an allotment of $206,481 from the federal government. The federal funds would come from the year-old Federal Road Act, passed the year before to aid state highway projects as a way to develop a national road system. Included in the bill was the first federal gasoline tax designed to be used for highway construction and maintenance. Yet this money was sparsely distributed to the states.

"Surveys have been made on state highway routes to determine the best and most economical location," the Highway Commission soon reported, "also, several important bridges have been designed and constructed."

Thus, the formation of the Oregon State Highway Commission was the first and most important step in building better roads for Oregon in general and for the coast in particular. "Get Oregon out of the Mud" became the slogan for its operation, which was eventually helped along by America's growing involvement in World War I.

After Congress declared war on Germany in 1917, some Oregonians feared a German invasion of America's western shore. Consequently, in September of that same year the Eugene Chamber of Commerce endorsed a plan "urging the immediate appropriation of funds [by the U.S. Congress] for the survey of a military highway from the Canadian border to the Mexican line."

The Pacific Coast Defense League had a plan and a route already in mind. It would stretch from Blaine, Washington to San Diego, California. On the southern Oregon coast, Coos Bay was quick to endorse the plan. That same year, I.S. Smith, a state senator representing Coos and Curry counties, proposed a petition to the Oregon State Legislature urging Congress to build a coast highway.

"The people of the Pacific Coast States," stated Smith's petition, "urgently request the building and maintaining of a military highway along the Pacific Coast from the Canadian border to the Mexi-

Building a plank highway along the Oregon coast, Tillamook County, 1914

can border for military necessities and defense such as supplying coast forts with guns and ammunition, the handling of artillery, ammunition and mobilizing troops in the event of an invasion."

In March of 1918, Oregon Governor James Withycombe called for the speedy completion of the military highway as a defensive measure. "I am reliably informed," he said, "that there are 250,000 trained German troops in Mexico and South America."

In addition to the military preparedness endorsed by highway proponents, residents of the coast knew that better roads meant expanded markets. Fishing, logging, mining, and other Oregon industries would all profit from a highway system that would permit transporting some of their products by automobile rather than by ship. This in turn would create both jobs and prosperity. And thanks to the automotive-craze, another boost to the economy was the expansion of tourism across the nation, especially in scenic wonderlands such as those found along the coastal frontiers of Oregon. People wanted to see the redwood forests, to take scenic drives along the beach, to fish and hunt. As a result, the coast highway became a powerful and popular idea across the state. The problem was how to build it.

At the time, two revolutionary industries affected the nation: making cars and building roads. But while automobiles were a private enterprise, roads were publicly-financed through local, state and federal government. To get this financing, the government needed a money source and a highway plan. But when the end of the war in 1918 brought an end to the idea for building a coastal military highway, individual states were left to their own resources. It soon became clear that Oregon's coastal communities urgently needed someone to spearhead the construction of a coast highway. They found that person in Benjamin F. Jones.

Benjamin F. Jones

Early in his life, B. F. Jones learned about the importance of good roads. After his mother, his only living parent, died of pneumonia when he was sixteen, Jones lived alone on his family's 160-acre coastal homestead in what was then part of Benton County. His first job was delivering mail, sometimes on horseback and sometimes by foot, on a muddy route that took him through much of Benton County from Toledo to Corvallis—and it was his experiences in that mud that made him a champion for decent roads.

A man of vision and intellect with a compulsion to pursue goals he considered worthwhile, Jones approached Benton County officials with the idea of improving the roads along the coast. But when they ridiculed his idea by calling coastal inhabitants a bunch of "clam diggers," Jones, at age thirty-five, began fighting to split Benton County into two counties.

With the help of coastal dignitaries, he succeeded in forming Bay County in 1893, though the name was changed later to Lin-

Plank and mud road along the Toledo-Newport mail route, early twentieth century

coln County by Senator Cogswell of Oregon, a Civil War veteran and admirer of Abraham Lincoln.

Jones went on to earn a law degree from Oregon Agricultural College and in 1897 was admitted to the Oregon Bar. After stints serving as mayor of Toledo and Newport and working as a lawyer, a saw mill operator, and a real estate developer, he was to achieve his greatest legacy in the state legislature as a representative of Lincoln and Polk counties.

In 1919 Jones authored a legislative proposal that provided the framework for naming and building the Oregon coast highway. The name came when ex-president Theodore Roosevelt died in January of that year, and Jones championed the passage of a house bill "to provide for the construction of a highway to be known as the Roosevelt Coast Military Highway, to be located from the city of Astoria...to the California state line."

The road was "to be owned, constructed and maintained by the United States," the bill explained, with the federal and state governments each appropriating $2.5 million for its construction. With the passage of this legislation, the matter was then put before Oregon voters for their approval. If passed, the new law would set in motion a chain of events that would make Oregon's coast a place accessible to everyone. Jones, sometimes referred to as the "Father of the Roosevelt Highway," campaigned tirelessly for the law's enactment. "Every public spirited citizen of every coast county should vote yes," said the *Coos Bay Times*, "and thus help in putting Oregon on the map."

The election was held on June 3, 1919, and two days later the results were in. "ROOSEVELT ROAD WINS," exclaimed the headline of the *Coos Bay Times*.

"The Roosevelt highway found favor almost everywhere," reported *The Oregonian*." Clackamas, Linn, Douglas, and Umatilla have the distinction of being the only counties…that have reported majorities against this proposal. The measure in the incomplete returns now has a majority in its favor of more than 21,000."

The people of Oregon had spoken: They wanted a coast highway. Now all they needed was the money to build it.

At Hug Point on the north Oregon coast, a wagon and an auto negotiate the beach highway at low tide.

Tillamook County officials involved with building the Roosevelt Highway, c.1920

Tillamook County road maintenance outfit, c. 1920

Tillamook County Road "Maintainer" c . 1920

Tillamook Court officials inspecting Tillamook River Bridge, near Weber residence, c. 1920

11

Tillamook rock crushing plant, c. 1920

Tillamook County road maintenance and road house, c. 1920

Oceanside plank road, c. 1920

Looking south on Oceanside Road, c. 1920

Nye Beach near Newport on the central Oregon coast in the 1920s.
White building at upper center is a natatorium, an indoor swimming pool
popular with tourists during the era.

Wrangling Funds
1919-1921

While waiting for the federal government to approve Oregon's request for $2.5 million in funding, the Oregon State Highway Commission achieved an unexpected coup: the enactment of the nation's first state gasoline tax—one cent per gallon. With 83,332 cars registered in Oregon at the time, this provided much-needed funding for road construction. It was a project that promised to be expensive because facing the department's engineers was the stark realization that up and down the coast of Oregon lay a rugged land with rocky bluffs, forested mountains, and numerous rivers, ravines, and gorges—all of which had to be either penetrated or crossed.

Furthermore, much of the approximately four hundred miles of coastline had yet to be surveyed. In fact, only about three miles of the *entire* Oregon coast was paved—a section south of Tillamook between Hemlock and Beaver. Beyond that, no roads existed on the central coast between Tillamook and Coos Bay, a distance of roughly 120 miles.

"I don't see," said a visitor struggling through the mud on the central coast, "how there can be any Christians where roads such as these exist!"

At the north and south ends, however, a road system of sorts *did* exist. Between Tillamook and Astoria in the north and between Coos Bay and Crescent City, California in the south, this

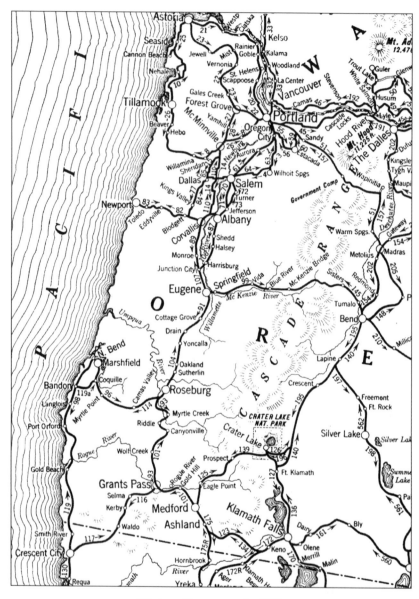

Western Oregon roads, 1920

16

system consisted of narrow roads that were rough-graded, wood-planked, or rock-covered as well as roads of bare dirt and open beach. These created a confusing network of routes that often led to dead ends and that always led drivers on real adventures. Take, for example, the 161-mile route from Coos Bay to Crescent City. "The route is especially interesting because of its diversity of scenery," said the 1920 *Automobile Blue Book*. "It follows alternately the rugged shore and inland road through dense virgin forests with occasional clearings for farming purposes."

Ben W. Olcott

But in finding that scenery, drivers encountered roads surfaced with planks, dirt, and gravel as they drove through numerous streams, crossed eight bridges, rode two ferries, and trundled over a variety of trestles built as dikes across marshes—all while following winding eight-foot-wide roadways with occasional ninety-degree turns through heavy forests and up steep headlands.

Albin W. Norblad

In addition, with rain making roads impassable and street lights yet to be invented, travel was reasonable only during the summer and then only during daylight hours. Even then, drivers in their open Tin Lizzies faced the elements with only a raincoat and goggles for protection. "Careful and prudent," was Oregon's speed law of the time, "not to exceed 30 miles per hour." Such was the condition of the southern part of the proposed Roosevelt Highway in 1920.

Road on the northern Oregon coast, Tillamook County, 1921

Road on the southern Oregon coast, Curry County, 1920

18

Yet the appeals of people along the coast for road construction money often fell on the seemingly-deaf ears of the Oregon Legislature, the Highway Commission, or Governor Ben W. Olcott. Portlanders, on the other hand, were often successful in their appeals for the same state funds. When the February 1, 1921 deadline for the federal government to approve its share of the funding arrived without the money, and when the U.S. Congress postponed for two years its decision about providing any funding at all, things looked bleak.

While coastal inhabitants watched the support of the legislature and the Highway Commission go to the other four highways, all they could do was dig their heels into the mud and persevere. Eventually, it paid off.

Early in 1921, Albin W. Norblad and Charles Hall, state senators who represented the coast, introduced the Norblad-Hall Roosevelt Military Highway Bill "to make [state] funds for the construction of the Roosevelt Military Highway available regardless of any federal appropriations." Passing the bill in the state senate, however, required some political scheming and maneuvering.

Two years earlier when B.F. Jones had first succeeded in getting approval for his highway bill, he and other westside legislators had also supported a measure that helped eastern Oregon farmers get loans for irrigation projects. Now the senators from the coast needed the same kind of support from those east of the Cascades.

"Oregon has signally failed in not showing the proper spirit of cooperation among its own population," Charles Hall said. "The people of southwestern Oregon voted for an irrigation measure of importance to eastern Oregon, though the southwest district has no more use for irrigation than a wagon has for five wheels."

Norblad added that "he had once heard from a savant of the east to the effect that some day the Pacific Coast would be the front door of the American continent and the Atlantic Coast the back door."

19

At the end of his speech, he emphasized the commercial productivity the coast could offer if only it had the highway to transport goods. After these two eloquent speakers finished, the senate voted unanimously for the bill, which then went to the house for a vote. But before it got there, it ran into trouble.

At a Highway Commission hearing on February 3, Chairman Booth vigorously opposed the Hall-Norblad plan. The next day, Senator Vinton moved to recall the Roosevelt bill from the house. The motion was seconded, but the final vote on the recall was moved to the following Monday because Senator Hall was in Coos Bay and would not return until then. When Monday came, the Senate voted 18-12 to recall the bill over the bitter protests of Norblad and Hall.

"You men and not I should be defending this bill," Hall said. "If this bill is not passed, I will do all in my power to prevent $2.5 million being placed into the general fund."

In essence, this meant that no other county could use these funds until the U.S. government signed off on the bill—and that was not likely to happen soon. The threat worked. Soon after Hall's speech, the senate reversed itself and again passed the highway bill. By the end of February, Governor Olcott signed a law "to declare and designate the Roosevelt Coast Military Highway as a state highway and to provide for the improvement of the same by the State Highway Commission."

The Roosevelt Highway would soon be on the Oregon map, even though the state's original request for $2.5 million of federal money was never authorized. Other federal funds, however, were sent to Oregon for building the state's highways, and it was the job of the Highway Commission to divide this money among the counties. Thus, the major share of financing for Oregon's highways during this period came first from the state, then from the federal government, and finally from Oregon counties.

In order to ensure that coastal communities got their share of funds, an organization called the Roosevelt Highway Association formed. Its first president was B.F. Jones, and the association eventually became one of the catalysts that fought for funding during the long road to the highway's completion.

By April of 1921, one completed segment of the highway ran seventeen miles inland between Coos Bay and Coquille, south of the old Coos Bay Wagon Road. The new road was sixteen-feet wide, included more than fifteen miles of concrete paving six-inches thick, and cost approximately $30,000 per mile to build.

"One of the great historical days of Coos County," the *Coos Bay Times* said of the highway's completion.

Coquille declared a holiday and organized the Highway Celebration, which featured Governor Olcott, state Highway Commission dignitaries, and State Senator Charles Hall. The day's festivities lasted into the night, and included a parade, a tug of war between Coos Bay and Coquille with "ten men to a side" and a prize of ten dollars, a 100-yard free-for-all race with a fifteen dollar prize, a band concert, and dancing "All day and Night,

Completed highway between Coos Bay and Coquille, shown here 1923

open air platform and two halls." And even though state officials promised in their speeches that the highway *would* be completed, more than 380 miles of it still remained to be built. This included finishing the rest of the Coos Bay Wagon Road to Roseburg, where it would turn southwest until reaching Crescent City, forming a highway "loop" through rugged and often wet terrain.

"A week ago the rains put the Coos Bay Wagon Road to Roseburg in rather bad shape," the *Coos Bay Times* reported that June, soon after the Coquille celebration. "The trip to Roseburg should not be attempted now…unless it is absolutely necessary and the driver willing to do some strenuous work…The rains have made the highway from Bandon south through Curry County very heavy.

In the 1920s, the Cadillac of ferries in the region was probably the *Tourist I* (shown here), the first ferry to cross the mouth of the Columbia River between Oregon and Washington. Completed in May of 1921, it was the first in a line of ferries operated by Astoria's Captain Fritz S. Elfving. His later versions carried as many as twenty-eight cars. In 1928 the *Tourist I* moved to Coos Bay, where it was used for about four years before moving again to Florence.

Woods Ferry across the Big Nestucca River, c.1920

Machines can get through but right now it is not a pleasant trip."

Besides rain and mud, another impediment to the flow of increased traffic were the ferries, which at the time were the only means of crossing coastal rivers and bays. Probably the most crude ferry of the day was the kind that drifted with the current and was then pulled back by a cable attached to a gasoline-powered winch, such as the one that crossed the Coquille River north of Bandon. Others consisted of tug-towed barges and even canoe-propelled small rafts. Only the largest ferries, however, could carry as many as fifteen cars—many carried just one or two—and the resulting long, slow lines hindered the flow of traffic. Even worse, unpredictable tides, bad weather, and high water could stop service for days or even weeks. A ferry operating out of Coos Bay at the time was the *Roosevelt*.

"This ferry has been completed," the *Coos Bay Times* reported in December of 1921, "and will operate between North Bend and Glasgow to give access to the road extending north of the bay toward Reedsport."

Southern loop, 1920

The *Roosevelt*, which could carry between twelve and nineteen cars and was powered by a two-cylinder, seventy-five horsepower steam engine, went immediately into service to help alleviate the increasing number of cars crossing the bay. In 1912, for example, 4,487 horse-drawn vehicles and 342 autos reportedly crossed the bay (a 13-1 ratio); while in 1921, with the *Roosevelt* making a crossing once per hour during summer days—winter roads on the coast were still too muddy for travel—auto traffic increased more than *twenty times* (to 6,979 cars) while horse-drawn vehicles dropped by more than half (to 2,214). This dramatic growth in automobile numbers continued to clog the ferry system up and down the coast through the 1920s.

Meanwhile, farther north, crews were also working on a north coast loop that incorporated the current road running between Tillamook and Astoria. "76.0 miles, via Seaside," is how the *Automobile Blue Book* described part of

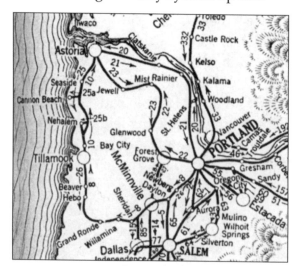

Northern loop, 1920

the route. "First 30 miles gravel, then 10 miles of graded dirt road across the mountains. This latter stretch is in good shape when dry, but during the rainy season will be very difficult to traverse; hard surface paving between Seaside and Astoria."

From Astoria the road followed the Columbia River to Portland, where it turned southwest and headed back to Tillamook. "From Portland down [to Astoria] it is a revelation," Leon Hirsch wrote that July in *The Oregonian*, "to my belief [it is] even grander than the section between here and Hood River [on the Columbia River Gorge Highway]."

The Scotch broom blossoming beside the road between Warrenton and Seaside prompted Hirsch to name it the Golden Highway. "It is not in hedges, but there are immense fields, acres of it," he wrote. "At no other place I have ever seen does it approach such luxuriance."

About the same time, another motorist-writer was heading in the opposite direction on the northern loop—southwest from Portland and toward Tillamook. "Beyond Sheridan and Willamina...It is this stretch of some fifty odd miles to Tillamook which is truly a sportsman's paradise," Henry R. Hayek wrote that summer in *The Oregon Motorist*. "Along these wonderful streams...one may feel the joy and thrill of actually being part of nature itself. In many places these camping spots are set in the very heart of the primeval forest—among giant trees...This is what the new Tillamook Highway offers every man, woman, and child...the tourists resting place: and a temple of worship for those who understand nature's teachings."

As the highway's scenery became more widely-publicized, it became the lure that began attracting more and more tourists. Armed with glamorous stories from adoring travelers, highway boosters tried to influence officials into investing more money

25

into their treasured Roosevelt Highway. But after touting the completion in 1921 of the Youngs Bay Bridge near Astoria, a major accomplishment on the highway, the Oregon State Highway Commission went back to putting their money into the state's other highways.

Youngs Bay Bridge—a drawbridge—1921

Beach at Pacific City, 1920s

Downtown Newport, 1920s

Kilchis River Bridge under construction, Tillamook County area, c. 1920

Wilson River Bridge, Tillamook County area, c. 1920

Starting Work
1922-1924

The terrain, labor, and expense involved in road construction on the coast ensured that the Roosevelt Highway proceeded slowly in 1922. After the surveyors scouted and plotted the routes, machines powered by horses or gas or steam gouged their way through brush, rocks, and trees. Then the grading of the road bed began, one of the most expensive jobs, draining off as much as thirty percent of the total budget. It was also one of the most important jobs.

The graded bed had to hold the surfacing materials, drain adequately, and be properly aligned and safely graded, preferably at slopes of no more than five percent. In addition, all curves were banked while wooden guard rails were installed along sharp curves and high embankments. The width of the roads varied from sixteen to twenty feet, depending on the amount of traffic it would receive. The busiest roads were paved in one of two ways. The first consisted of a six-inch foundation of macadam, compacted broken stones, covered with five inches of a bituminous pavement, generally consisting of a hot mixture of asphalt cement and an aggregate such as fine gravel ("blacktop"); the second was six to seven inches of concrete. Other roads were surfaced with gravel put down in two layers: four inches of coarse rocks topped with three-quarters of an inch of fine rock. Even graveled roads could cost as much as $6,000 per mile.

At the end of 1922, the total 408-mile length of the Roosevelt

Caterpillar and crew clearing snags from the Roosevelt Highway, Tillamook County, 1922

Highway from Astoria to the California border had just over fifty-nine miles of pavement and sixty-four miles of rock and gravel, with another fifteen miles graded and ready for surfacing. As far as the other 270 miles of it was concerned, engineers and construction crews struggled to improve, even move, these primitive routes. On the south coast, one such road led inland and north from Brookings. It followed a steep ridgeline to a point about halfway to Gold Beach at Pistol River.

"The road was unsurpassed anywhere in the world for hazards of rocks, tree roots, and bogs," one newspaper reported. "Often enough autoists, upon meeting another vehicle, were compelled to back half a mile or more to find a place wide enough for passing."

The Highway Commission wanted to move this ridgeline road farther west to follow the coastline. "[The present road] is danger-

Downtown Bandon, Oregon, 1920s

ous and hardly passable even in the summer," a surveyor reported. "The country needs the [new] road badly...It is logical to as-
sume that there should be the best route close to the coast...There
are no good maps of this section...The country is very rough and
rugged and covered with thick brush."

Despite the obstacles, the growing number of motorists along
the southern coast's loop road brought an expanding tourist trade
to the region.

"Greatest Out Door Playground on the Pacific Coast Opened
by New System of Roads Penetrating Coos and Curry Counties," stated a headline of the *Coos Bay Times*. "Around the Rogue
River and to the south are found the azaleas, which are seen by
the thousands," said the accompanying article. "There are whole
fields of them and they vary in color from lovely salmon pink
to white. The abundance of wild flowers is particularly promi-
nent between Corbin and Rogue River. There are not just a few
flowers in places, but great masses...a continuous panorama of
bright colors."

Even though the roads were still undeveloped, sometimes even downright dangerous, and usually accessible only during the summer, entrepreneurs along the route began building auto campgrounds, rental cottages, general stores, gas stations, garages, hotels, eateries, and fishing and hunting resorts.

"Curry County," reported the *Coos Bay Times*, "formerly an isolated but rich territory, has been opened by the Roosevelt Highway."

As the highway progressed, communities such as Bandon—then with a population of approximately 1,500—prospered. Rentals were scarce and local industries included two salmon canneries, a number of sawmills, and probably the nation's largest condensed milk factory, which employed 125 people at the height of its production. The town was typical of many coastal communities in that some of its residents claimed the opening of the Roosevelt Highway "was the most important single development of the year." They were also typical in what they had to offer the rush of tourists drawn to the area: beaches and views, fishing and hunting, and even large natatoriums, indoor swimming pools sometimes filled with heated sea water.

Farther south, Californians couldn't wait to try out their new autos over the northern routes. Consequently, at this point on the southern loop, spring brought not only the glorious fields of wild flowers, but also the trundling tourists with their visions of wondrous holidays.

Meanwhile, people on Oregon's northern loop were also counting on a big influx of tourists, waiting for the burgeoning trade from Portland and points farther east. But then on a December day in 1922, these expectations came crashing to a halt when a fire devastated Astoria. The blaze wiped out two dozen blocks of the city, burning businesses to the ground and causing an estimated $12 million in damages.

"Offers of assistance are pouring into Astoria from many sources," reported the *Daily Astorian*. "Expressions of sympathy are taking practical forms. The entire Northwest is showing a fine spirit in regard to assisting us in the midst of trouble…Astoria is thankful…let the thanks of the community be extended to these generous ones."

Images of people hungry, homeless, and out of work filled Oregon newspapers. One thing that helped these people, however, was the employment available on the Roosevelt Highway. Thus, it was discovered that the Roosevelt Highway could not only attract tourists' dollars, but also offer help during times of economic hardship. And as highway construction continued, the nation's growing love affair with the automobile showed no signs of slowing down.

In 1923, production of automobiles in the U.S. reached 3,780,358. These included Buicks, Chevrolets, Dodges, and even the Model A Deusenberg, in styles ranging from coupes to sedans and from trucks to tractors. Other vehicles of the day traversing the rocky, narrow roads were busses—referred to as "stages"—

Astoria after the fire, 1922

Cleared right of way for the Roosevelt Highway, Tillamook county, 1922

made by Studebaker and Packard, with the Astoria–Seaside Stage Line making a round trip six times a day. But the most popular car by far was the Ford, which was approaching the manufacture of its ten millionth car.

"The demand for automobiles during 1923 will be greater than during any other year," said Edsel B. Ford president of the Ford Motor Company. "There are hundreds of thousands of potential owners in all parts of the country who have yet to buy their first car."

More cars, of course, required more and better roads—especially along the Oregon coast. "Before the finish of my term in office," Governor Walter M. Pierce said in a 1923 speech, "I believe we will see its [Roosevelt Highway] completion."

Pushed by the governor to finish, the Oregon State Highway Commission reported they had spent more money on the

Planked Main Street in Rockaway, Tillamook county, 1920s

Roseburg-Coos Bay Highway, 1920s

Percheron horse pulling a fresno during construction of the Oregon Coast Highway near Garibaldi, 1927

Roosevelt than on any other highway in the state. (Of the $3 million spent on the highway in 1923 and 1924, $1.7 million had come from the state, $700,000 from the federal government, and $600,000 from Oregon counties.) In spite of this assertion, the Pacific Highway was completed in 1923, and The Dalles-California Highway was progressing at a faster pace than the coast highway.

Cloverdale Stage on the north Oregon coast, 1920s

Small sections of the Roosevelt, however, were getting finished, though some thought it was happening at a snail's pace. These sections included three miles of improved grading and surfacing between Seaside and Cannon Beach Junction, and another five miles between Mohler and the northern Tillamook County line. In addition, the new Lewis and Clark Bridge—a draw bridge over the Lewis and Clark River three miles south of Astoria and costing approximately $190,000—was nearing completion. Meanwhile, on July 3, 1924, the city of Astoria, resurrected from the fire's ruin, celebrated the "New Astoria Reconstruction Celebration: From Ashes to Concrete."

With more miles of roads, more cars on those roads, and Prohibition in full swing, an increase in traffic accidents seemed inevitable. "Accidents have been somewhat frequent lately on the highways," the *Coos Bay Times* reported, "but in most every case they have been due to breaking the speed limits, utter carelessness, or the driver having indulged too freely in moonshine."

The rugged road along the Oregon coast was part of the appeal to some intrepid travelers. The cautious driver of the early 1920s had to have a mechanical aptitude and be ready to face all obstacles that lay in his path. Necessities he packed along included automotive tools, extra tires, tire pump, tire patching equipment, tire chains, shovel and pick, and rain gear. In addition, drivers needed a great supply of self-reliance and resourcefulness in dealing with misfortune.

"Five persons narrowly escaped serious injury yesterday afternoon when a touring car in which they were riding went off the Fairview Road and rolled completely over," one newspaper said about an accident near Coquille in August of 1924. "They put the machine back on the road and drove on. The only damage done was the wrecking of the top and windshield."

Winter roads, of course, posed an even greater threat to drivers and their cars. In November of 1924, for example, one section of the southern coast loop experienced some bad slides. "Eugene

Muddy and steep road typical along the Oregon coast before the building of the highway

Chadwick...came near being marooned on the Roseburg-Coos Bay Highway Sunday on account of the storm," reported a newspaper. "Not only were there slides in front of them but several occurred back of them...Mr. Chadwick and companions got out and wielded pick and shovel assisting the road crews to clear."

The year 1924 also saw the completion of another section of the Roosevelt Highway, one finally penetrating the central coast by running between Neskowin in Tillamook County and the Siletz River in Lincoln County. This new route, the *Yaquina Bay News* reported, "will give the first all-year road outlet that part of the county has ever had in the past, for nine or ten months of the year. [Before this,] they could get out only by walking, horseback or by four horse team."

Yet one major concern of people living on the coast was the long unfinished section stretching between the Siletz River and Coos Bay. "In southwestern Lincoln and western Lane and Douglas counties," the Highway Commission reported in 1924, "there has been no improvement on the Roosevelt Highway."

At the end of 1924, 60 miles of the highway were paved, 136 miles were graded and surfaced with rock or gravel, and 18 miles were graded and ready for surfacing. In two years, crews had developed seventy-six miles of highway but paved just one of them. What was left was 194 narrow, crooked miles, almost half the total length, and the beaches were still used as roads over much of that distance.

But like the city of Astoria, which resurrected itself from the fire's ruin to celebrate its rebuilding in 1924, the Roosevelt Highway seemed destined to continue.

Construction of a plank road underway along the Oregon coast

Seeing Changes
1925-26

At the beginning of 1925, the Roosevelt Highway disappeared—at least, it's name did at the national level. Aware that the current system of road names "was too cumbersome," the federal government that year decided to eliminate the confusion by undertaking "immediately the selection and designation of a comprehensive system of through interstate routes." These routes would total less than three percent of all the nation's highways, and E. W. James, member of the Joint Board of Interstate Highways, was placed in charge of creating the system.

"With the north south roads numbered odd from east to west," James said, "and the east west roads numbered even from north to south, you at once start a simple systematic, complete, and expansible pattern for a long time development."

This became the national standard by which roads were named. For example, the Lincoln Highway, which ran from Astoria to Atlantic City as the first transcontinental highway, became U.S. Highway 30, while the highway along the coast between the Canadian border and the Mexican line became U.S. Highway 101—except in Oregon, where, the segment of the coast highway that lay within the state's borders remained the Roosevelt Highway.

In addition to the new numbering system, interstate routes adopted U.S. Standard Road Markers and Signs. The idea was that standard designs for crucial roads signs—such as the rectan-

Walter M. Pierce

gular information sign, the round train-crossing sign, and the octagonal stop sign—would make them more recognizable to drivers, and thus prevent traffic accidents and save lives.

Another change in 1925 was that the state of Oregon attempted to clear the bottlenecks created by the ferries along the coast by building its own system along the highway. In February of that year, Oregon Governor Walter Pierce signed a law authorizing the State Highway Commission "to establish, acquire, construct, maintain and operate a ferry across any stream, river, bay, arm of the ocean or other body of water on a state highway." The law, however, would not be put to practical use for two more years.

Sadly, 1925 was also the year Oregon lost Benjamin F. Jones, "Father of the Roosevelt Highway," who on March 9 died of a heart attack. Yet his vision for the road continued as the highway progressed and other developments followed. For example, one Portlander traveling the northern loop that year through Astoria to Tillamook described some of the wonders he discovered along the way—the hotel and golf course at Gearhart, the natatorium at

Hotel Gearhart

Seaside, the "succulent" shell fish and good fishing on the beaches. And always, there was the wonder of the road itself.

"Along a portion of the paved highway leading from Astoria to Gearhart and Seaside," he wrote, "the road becomes a narrow

Once there lived a man of vision
Of a thing that was to be.
T'was a highway for the nation
Built along the western sea.
And this thing he daily dreamed of
Till he saw it all unfold
As a thing of wondrous beauty
Then his dream to others told.
There were some who doubtless
Laughed him
All to scorn for such a thought,
That a highway here was needed
They had not the vision caught.
But his spirit was undaunted
And he spent his gold and time
For the good of all the nation
For the vision was sublime.
Tho one day death came and took him
He had lived to see the gleam
Of the work that he had started
Other men had caught his dream.
So within our hearts we hold him
As we stop and meditate
Worthy of the praise we give him
He is numbered with the great.

Charles A. Ewing
Tribute to Benjamin F. Jones
Newport Journal, September 14, 1927

lane…hedged in by golden blossoms of miles of Scotch Broom. Other stretches are shadowed by towering firs…it zigzags downward on the other side in a forest of giant trees where but rarely the sun breaks through the dense canopy of branches, [and on the beach] you may speed your car at miles an hour on the hard sand with scarcely a vibration."

With reports of such grandeur circulating in newspapers and magazines, even more people began crowding onto the Roosevelt Highway. Now all the state had to do was finish it.

"Complete the Roosevelt Highway Within Three Years," became the slogan of the Roosevelt Highway Association. Governor Pierce, however, declared that $7 million was needed to finish the project, a sum he thought could not be raised "in less than seven years." He listed as some of the expenses "heavy construction, slides, bridges, the difficulty of obtaining rock surface material, and the excessive cost of getting in supplies."

As if to prove his point, a small disaster soon struck part of the highway. "Another slide took place Tuesday evening on the Roosevelt Coast Highway between Otter Rocks and Rocky Creek," an engineer reported in August of 1925, "completely blocking the road and covering the steam shovel with about eight feet of dirt and rock and leaving it at such an angle that it may slide into the canyon becoming a total loss." The engineer predicted it would take at least a month to clear the road. Despite these kinds of setbacks, progress on the highway continued slowly.

In 1926, for example, Arthur D. Sullivan, automobile editor for *The Oregonian*, and a friend drove the entire route from Astoria to Crescent City. Along the way, the two ran into numerous difficulties, including rain and mud, construction delays and lengthy detours, and necessary rescues from soft sand and mud holes—but they made the trip in a total time of fifty-seven hours. This was only six hours longer for the entire 408-mile drive than George A. Laffaw's ill-fated 161-mile journey just eight years earlier.

That same year, Californians heading north to try out their

Highway and redwood forest near Crescent City, 1920s

new Model T Fords on the southern loop noted other improvements when six miles north of the border they crossed the new
steel Chetco River Bridge. Farther north, they arrived at Brookings, where all non-residents were now required to register their

New grade on the Roosevelt Highway south of Gold Beach, 1923

vehicles, at no cost, with the Highway Commission. Here they could also obtain a list of traffic regulations.

"The speed limits for passenger vehicles," said one regulation, "are as follows: 30 miles per hour outside of the corporate limits of cities and towns; 20 miles per hour at junctions and intersections, and within the corporate limits of cities and towns; 12 miles per hour past school houses." In addition, Oregon drivers, who now numbered approximately 215,000, had to obtain the new Certificate of Title for their automobiles, whether it was a passenger car, truck, bus, or farm vehicle.

As drivers proceeded north on gravel and dirt, they eventually turned on to the ridgeline road—provided sunny weather prevailed—that led to the small farming town of Carpenterville before dropping down to the Pistol River on the coast, midway between Brookings and Gold Beach. Looking south from that point, they might have seen horse-drawn scrapers clearing the new highway, a steam shovel digging at the road's edge, or a steamroller smashing rocks of the roadbed. Once at Gold Beach, they proceeded about five miles upstream to cross the Rogue River on Bagnell's Ferry. From there it was on to the Arizona Inn for food or a room.

The next stop, after winding over Humbug Mountain, was Port Orford. If motorists stayed at one of the new auto camps, and if they liked seafood and were prepared to cook for themselves, they had no problem finding something to eat. Hunting along the beach at low tide could produce rock oysters, razor clams, crabs, and mussels. Some campers collected murr eggs, while still others fished for salmon, cod, or halibut.

North of Port Orford they would have come upon the lighthouse at Cape Blanco, the westernmost point in the United States. The light house overlooked a reef that extended for hundreds of feet into the Pacific Ocean and was covered with thousands of gulls and hundreds of sea lions.

"The reef affords a playground for sea lions," reported a *Coos Bay Times* of the day, "and hunters oftentimes kill hundreds of them in a few hours."

After crossing the Sixes River, drivers could encounter slow-moving trucks hauling mining equipment to the Big Placer

Roosevelt Highway near Port Orford, Humbug Mountain in the distance

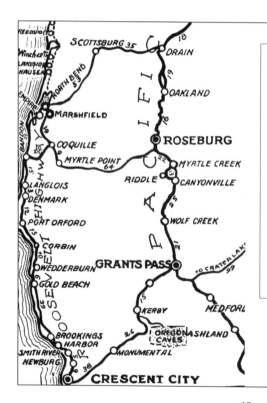

The Roosevelt Highway Route

The southern section of the Roosevelt Highway extending from North Bend, Oregon to Crescent City, California, passing a short distance from Cape Blanco, the most westerly point in the United States, derives its title, "Out Where the West Ends".

Skirting the Pacific Ocean for the greater distance it is unsurpassed in scenic beauty, passing through millions of feet of big standing timber, and where hunting and fishing abound throughout a section of the country which enjoys the most equitable climate in America.

You will never regret an auto trip over this route where every spot is a camping spot.

Postcard from 1920s shows the route (left) and describes the wonders along the southern portion of the Roosevelt Highway.

Mine—the largest gold mine in the country—huge logs to local sawmills, or even ten gallon milk cans to the cheese factories farther north. Then it was on to Bandon, Coquille, and Coos Bay. From there, motorists turned east to Roseburg to finish the loop back to Crescent City.

Meanwhile, the stretch connecting the central coast to the northern was also progressing. "[The] Roosevelt Highway," reported a 1926 issue of the *Newport Journal*, "will be ready some time this coming season from Newport clear through to the Columbia River."

Another stretch of road on the central coast, one that connected with the highway, had just nine miles left to finish. Thirty-five miles long, it started at Newport, led east to Toledo near the head of Yaquina Bay, then turned north to follow the Siletz River to Kernville on Siletz Bay (today's Highway 229). Any driver taking this stretch, said the *Newport Journal*, would pass through "the largest belt of standing spruce in the state or perhaps the nation [but] already the logging operations have spoiled the beauty of part of this route."

Yet it was this same logging that had some calling Toledo "the busiest town in Lincoln County," with the sawmill there, the Pacific Spruce Corporation, said to be the largest in the world, producing more lumber per day than any other mill in the nation. Even so, the *Newport Journal* proposed that the federal government purchase a strip of timber "twenty-five to fifty feet, along each side of the road," which would not only protect the area's beauty, but also produce greater revenue through tourism." Evi-

Pacific Spruce Corporation in Toledo, reputedly the biggest sawmill in the world at the time

Roosevelt Highway at entrance to Coos Bay, 1923

dently, it was a plan too far ahead of its time.

By the end of 1926, the Oregon State Highway Commission reported that the largest share of funds available to them had been poured into building of the Roosevelt Highway. "Of the $3,320,720 expended," the commission wrote, "the state has contributed $2,163,305, the federal government has contributed $855,869, and the counties have contributed $300,789."

Of the total mileage covered by the highway, 58 miles were now paved, 10 miles were surfaced with oiled macadam, 180 miles were

---

Length of the Roosevelt Highway by Year

1921-22: 409 miles

1923-24: 408 miles

1925-26: 405 miles

1927-28: 405 miles

1929-30:395 miles

(From the Biennial Reports of the
Oregon State Highway Commission)

surfaced with crushed rock and gravel, and 63 miles were graded and ready for surfacing. (No explanations were given for the two-mile reduction in pavement from two years before, but the three-mile shortening of the total length was typical because the overall route seemed to shrink as improvements continued.) This meant that more than seventy percent of the highway was ready to use, with less than ninety-four miles left to finish.

Roosevelt Highway skirting Humbug Mountain outside Port Orford, 1920s

Roosevelt Highway in northern Curry County, 1920s

Resolving Differences
1927-1929

In 1927, the grading and surfacing of the southern loop was at last finished. In August at Gold Beach, officials cut the ribbon and opened what residents believed was the beginning of a bright future. The following month on the central coast, another vital section of the highway opened at a dedication ceremony held before an estimated one thousand people at Lincoln County's Rocky Creek Bridge. The 360-foot bridge, which spanned a small gorge ten miles north of Newport and near Otter Crest, was dedicated to the vision and labor of the late Benjamin F. Jones. When Lorraine Jones, his four-year-old granddaughter, cut the ribbon, this portion of the Roosevelt Highway was declared officially open to the public.

Rocky Creek Bridge, 1929

"It is up to the people of Lincoln County," Highway Commissioner H.B. Van Duzer said at the dedication ceremony, "to prevent its being spoiled by hot dog stands and such commercial ventures that are repulsive to the better class of travelers."

Yet not all coast citizens were happy with how the work was progressing. As auto traffic along the coast increased and the highway improved, long lines at ferry crossings continued to hinder travel. And as the crescendo of voices grew louder against these slow-moving ferries, the Highway Commission finally took action. In 1927 it assumed control of ferries at Gold Beach, Coos Bay, Reedsport, Florence, Waldport, and Newport. It was now the state's job to create a free ferry system across the remaining unbridged rivers and bays, with the idea of building bridges at these same locations in the future.

Conde B. McCullough

As a part of the new system, the state contract called for ferrymen to wear "pretty uniforms." Seamen were required to wear "a suit of blue" in the winter and "white trousers and blue coat" in the summer. In addition, "the ferry boat must be kept spick and span at all times, and the attendants must use every courtesy to the patrons." For this service, ferry owners received $1,500 a month.

Safety was also an issue. "At the foot of each ferry landing we are going to erect a substantial timber fence painted white and equipped with a suitable 'Stop' sign," bridge engineer Conde B. McCullough wrote for the Highway Commission. "This fence will be reinforced by means of a system of heavy cables so that it will be utterly impossible for a car to crash through."

Besides the ferries, another problem was the unfinished road itself. One critic from the coast wrote to the *Newport Journal* that the highway was "two uncompleted ends that go nowhere," and that if Benjamin F. Jones were still alive "his message would not be of epitaphs or monuments, but the thundering charge to his people, 'fight lest they rob you of your birthright!'"

Communities along the coast voiced similar frustrations through their legislative representatives, who clamored for the Highway Commission to sell more bonds. You've built the Pacific Highway and The Dalles Highway, they said, and now its time to complete the coast highway. "We'll have the highway finished in three years," Van Duzer promised, then offered a list of accomplishments, including the completion of numerous bridges.

"The Soapstone Creek Bridge in Clatsop County," he wrote, "the Nehalem River Bridge in Tillamook County, the Rocky Creek and Depoe Bay Bridges in Lincoln County, the Schofield River Bridge in Douglas County and the Pistol River, Euchre Creek and Hunters Creek Bridges in Curry County."

Depoe Bay Bridge

Roosevelt Highway near Frankfort, south of Bandon in Curry County, c. 1930

Even though twenty percent of the highway remained unfinished along the central coast, with bridges still to be built over major rivers and bays, conditions along the route were steadily, if slowly, improving. This was a fact that Lawrence Barber, automobile editor for *The Oregonian*, proved in September of 1929 when he set out to better Arthur D. Sullivan's 1926 time of fifty-seven hours for driving the length of the coast.

Accompanied by three friends and driving two cars, a 1929 Marquette and a Buick sedan, Barber's goal was to drive the entire highway from Astoria to Crescent City in one day. "With good drivers, with good cars and good weather," Barber said, "[we] could make this difficult run in less than 24 hours—with good luck."

Leaving from the Hotel Astoria in dry weather and driving no more than the posted speed limit of thirty-five miles per hour over the mostly macadam-surfaced road, Barber and his friends made the first 155 miles to Newport in just over four hours. After crossing Yaquina Bay on the ferry, they drove into the unfinished gap between Newport and Reedsport, a stretch, Barber wrote, consisting of corduroy roads and hard-packed beach.

"We finished the 18 mile run to the Alsea River by gingerly driving for a fourth of a mile on a single lane timber trestle to the ferry landing," Barber wrote. "The trestle consisted of two tracks, flanged on the inside, and elevated about 15 feet above the sand by pilings...The ferry crossing to Waldport was a 15 minute voyage, costing us $1.80 per car. We had to detour from the ferry landing to town and had additional detours along the dirt road to Yachats. Next was an exciting single lane dirt road from Yachats to Florence for 33 miles...It wound around the ocean face of Cape Perpetua and Heceta Head...At times the trail was laid close to the beach: 10 minutes later it might be 500 feet up on a ledge of the bluffs, high above the pounding surf. We met only two cars on this wild road." (Should they have had to pass another auto, the law of the time stated the passing driver had to "give audible warning with his horn...before passing...a vehicle proceeding in the same direction.")

The two-car caravan finally reached the Heceta Head light-house near Florence. "Heavily timbered mountains rose all around us," Barber wrote. "We dropped down to Cape Creek, crossed a wooden bridge and climbed a 20 percent grade up the south side of Sea Lion Point...As we dropped down the south side of the mountain, we had a grand view of the sand dune des-ert stretching almost to Florence...The 41-mile run from Waldport to Florence required four hours and five minutes, an average of about 10 miles an hour."

The party crossed the Siuslaw River at Florence by ferry; it was their third ferry crossing. From Florence they drove inland on dry roads to Gardiner, where they continued south to the ferry at the Umpqua River. "[We] then boarded the...ferry for the two and one half mile crossing to Reedsport," Barber wrote. "The fer-

Cape Blanco Catholic Church, Curry County

ryman, A.F. Smith, collected 50 cents a car…We felt like pioneers. We had driven 244 miles in 13 and one half hours, compared with the 29 hours driven by Sullivan to this point. We had 173 miles yet to go to the California state line and 194 miles to Crescent City."

From Reedsport on, Barber wrote, it was "duck soup" for the travelers. The only inconvenience was their wait for the ferry at Wedderburn and "a winding dirt mountain road between Pistol River and Brookings." The group arrived at the Lauff Hotel in Crescent City just 21 hours and 15 minutes after their start in Astoria.

It was that middle, unfinished part of Barber's journey—the corduroy roads and hard-packed beaches—that had coast residents so up in arms, especially in Newport. The *Newport Journal* became a crusader in the fight to complete the highway, vigorously pushing the state to sell bonds, and calling for Governor Isaac Lee Patterson—the third governor to hold office since the highway was first approved in 1919—to back the plan. Both the

Isaac Lee Patterson

commission and the governor, however, said the sale of new bonds with the resulting increased indebtedness was not the solution, and that in time the road would be completed.

Spurring on the debate for the next two years were the glowing reports of increased tourism along the southern coast. "A gorgeous blaze of bloom," said a June 1929 issue of *The Oregon Motorist*, "a dazzling landscape, an ever changing panorama of thousands of wonderful vistas…from Marshfield 140 miles south to the Oregon-California state line."

On the southern coast: Roosevelt Highway and Rogue River near Wedderburn in Curry County, c. 1930

On the central coast: auto camp in Lincoln County, 1930

Other motorists had discovered more than the view. "Sportsmen throng lower Rogue River," reported a Curry County newspaper in October of 1929. "By far the largest crowd of sport fishermen ever to assemble on the Lower Rogue River in one day enjoyed the unexcelled sport fishing here on Sunday."

With increasing frequency, the *Newport Journal* pointed out the southern coast's huge increase in the tourist trade. "Tourists Swamp Hotels," it reported about Bandon. "Hotels and tourists camps are unable to accommodate the horde now passing up and down the coast."

The newspaper also compared the significant increase in out-of-state cars appearing in Oregon: "the Roosevelt Highway of over 59 per cent, The Dalles-California [Highway] 22 per cent, the Pacific [Highway] 8 per cent."

To publicize the situation more, a caravan of representatives from coastal cities traveled the highway from Astoria to Crescent City, and then drove back to Salem to meet with Governor Patterson, who told them that more than $5 million was funded for highway construction during the next year and a half. The governor did not, however, state how much of that money was specifically budgeted for the Roosevelt Highway.

Certainly, the Newport paper reasoned, the highway commission was aware that of the "17 percent" that coast residents paid for their "auto license" and gasoline taxes, the coast was entitled to have at least that amount of the construction budget go to their highway.

Finally, on October 19, 1929, the governor told a coast delegation that enough money was available for the coming year, intimating that the Roosevelt Highway was high on his priority list. Maybe they at last had made progress, the coast highway boosters believed; maybe the governor would follow through on his promises; maybe the highway would be finished with no more delays, no more setbacks. Then, ten days later, all that changed.

October 29, 1929. Black Tuesday. The stock market crash. The start of the Great Depression.

As if oblivious to America's tragedy, the federal government allocated to Oregon more than two million dollars for road construction—then announced the money was available only if the state could match it. But the governor kept his word.

"There is no question but that the Highway Commission will make use of every dollar of federal [funds] to Oregon," said Governor Patterson, "and if necessary, bonds will be sold to do so."

Patterson spurred the Highway Commission to resume work on the central portion of the highway, and initiated the building of a bridge over the Rogue River. Then in December of 1929, the governor caught a cold, went home to bed, and soon died of pneumonia.

As president of the State Senate, Albin W. Norblad of Astoria, one of the Roosevelt Highway's most active supporters, became the next governor, taking the oath of office on Christmas day, 1929.

As governor, Norblad left no doubt about one of his top priorities: He urged the sale of bonds to complete the Roosevelt Highway and to provide jobs for the unemployed. "I therefore recommend," he said, "an early completion of the present designed highways."

Spanning Rivers
1930-1932

Cutting the highway through forests and rock was one thing, but getting it across rivers and bays was something else. As 1930 began, some of the last, longest, and costliest bridges still had to be built. The first of these crossed the Rogue River.

Building the Rogue River Bridge was hailed as one of the last big steps in the completion of the highway as well as one of its grandest features. "Your bridge here will not only be the largest state highway bridge," H.B. Van Duzer said in a speech at Gold Beach, "but it will be one of the most beautiful in design."

Aerial view of the plan for the Rogue River Bridge, 1929

Rogue River Bridge, December 30, 1930

With seven graceful arches, the bridge would sweep across the river in grand style while supporting a road twenty-seven feet wide and pedestrian walkways on each side. In addition, four great obelisks would tower thirty feet above the road and contain lookouts where visitors could see the mouth of the mighty Rogue and the deep blue of the Pacific. Estimated to cost $600,000, the bridge

Rogue River Bridge, July 17, 1931

would be the largest contract awarded in 1930, and at 1,898 feet long, it would be the longest bridge on the West Coast between San Francisco Bay and the Columbia River. Furthermore, the enormous supplies of lumber, sand, gravel, and concrete demanded by the project would help the Gold Beach economy, which was suffering from tax foreclosures on properties and high unemployment.

In the first week of March 1930, work on the bridge began; by the end of the year, it had reached the midpoint mark. "Rogue River Bridge One-Half Finished," the *Curry County Reporter* stated in December. "Where there were 75 to 80 men working the past summer, next year there will be from 150 to 175."

During the construction of the bridge, however, some people began having second thoughts about the name of the Roosevelt Highway, deciding that Oregon Coast Highway might be more suitable, "Such a change in name it seems is desired," said the Portland Chamber of Commerce, "because of the fact that there is now a transcontinental highway called the Roosevelt Highway."

The *Curry County Reporter* claimed there were actually two other Roosevelt highways in America. "There is the Roosevelt Memorial Highway," the paper said, "an international highway...

One of two arched bridges between Cape Creek Bridge and Yachats, built in 1932

Cape Creek Bridge, north of Florence, OR

from Portland, Maine to Portland, Oregon; and there is another Roosevelt Highway in California…[Oregon Coast Highway] was the name best suited and the name the coast counties wanted and they got it." In February of 1931, the Oregon State Legislature made the new name official.

After the christening to Oregon Coast Highway, the race to complete the roadway and its bridges accelerated. Besides the Rogue River Bridge, five other bridges were under construction at the same time: four in Lane County—at Cummins Creek, Tenmile Creek, Big Creek, and Cape Creek—and one in Tillamook County across the Wilson River. Of these, the largest and most unique was the Cape Creek Bridge and Tunnel, located approximately twelve miles north of Florence.

When finished, this spectacular bridge would stretch 619 feet across the Cape Creek Gorge. "A single central arch will be 220 feet long, with a center rise of 94 feet," *The Oregonian* reported. "On both sides of the arch the roadway support will be provided by two series of aqueduct arches, six 40 foot arches on the bottom and twenty-eight 20 foot arches on the top.."

At the south end of the double-tiered structure, the highway would bore through Devils Elbow, penetrating 714 feet to create Cape Creek Tunnel. At a cost of more than $50,000, the tunnel's construction was a major undertaking.

"Three shifts of workers have been employed for months on the tunnel and the bore now reaches about 400 feet," the *Siuslaw Oar* reported in June of 1931. "When enough clearing has been made, three or four more crews will be employed here...There is a real village here of cabins and tents—men, women and children, for there are several camps in one." The nearby Roosevelt Highway Lumber Company supplied the lumber for the bridge, "Much of it being timbers of 50 or 60 feet in length."

The new bridge and tunnel made Florence an important city. Never in all the realm of any local activity," wrote the editor of the *Siuslaw Oar*, "had we ever beheld anything like it...it's beyond the ability of a country editor."

But of equal importance at the time was the construction of the Siuslaw Highway between Florence and Junction City near Eugene (part of today's Highway 126). "Thirty miles of first class oiled roads, a reporter for *The Oregonian* wrote after he had traveled west on the highway in june of 1931. An additional six miles brings the motorist to the end of the completed highway and to the beginning of the new construction."

Rogue River Bridge, January 13, 1932

One real estate developer proclaimed that the Siuslaw Highway made Florence not only centrally located on the Oregon Coast Highway, but also at the west end of a new transcontinental highway.

"The New York-Florence Highway crosses the North Fork on the draw bridge and leads up the main river to Eugene, thence eastward to New York City," he wrote. "These two great super highways comprise the 'Main Street' of the nation, from the Atlantic to the Pacific, and from Mexico to British Columbia." (He went on to explain that he had 800 acres with highway and lake frontage, prime residential and commercial sites, all at "nominal prices.")

The bridges and tunnel were not built without human costs. In April of 1931, for example a worker on the Rogue River Bridge was seriously hurt, said the *Curry County Reporter*, when "a block broke from a boom and struck him on the head...The man's condition is said to be critical."

In June, "Herb Woodin, Jr. tried to saw off one of his fingers... Emil Koski ran a carpenter's chisel between his thumb and forefinger of his left hand and severed an artery...Eric Kivst let a heavy timber fall on one of his ankles...Bill Chenoweth is a patient in the Gold Beach Hospital suffering from severe abdominal strains received while working on the Oregon [Coast] Highway near Port Orford."

In October, "Ed Cannon, aged about 45 years, lost his life Wednesday morning when footings gave while working on the side of a cliff near the sea lions cave north of Florence...and rolled down the steep incline for 300 feet and landed on the rocks at the edge of the sea." Another worker also fell, but caught a bush and was able to save himself.

In spite of these catastrophes, highway construction zoomed along. "[The] completion of the Tahkenitch, Heceta and Perpetua sectors," *The Oregonian* reported, "will provide a surfaced highway from the Columbia River to the California line."

In addition, an engineer for the Highway Commission wrote that "between Reedsport and Florence...There remains only four miles of grading." While north of Florence, "There are several grading and bridge contracts now underway, the completion date of which is set at December 31, 1931. The balance of the highway from Cape Perpetua northward to Tillamook is entirely completed."

One reason for the progress was that the state had authorized $1 million for major highway construction, and another $1 million for secondary roads. This money, said state officials, would be "distributed among the various counties, largely for hand work where need for employment is acute. Only heads of families or men with dependents and residents of the state for six months will be given work."

With more money and men at work on the coast, and with the Gold Beach Chamber of Commerce scheduling the dedication of the Rogue River Bridge in May of 1932, the State Highway Commission asserted that this would mark the completion of the Oregon Coast Highway, and both the bridge and the road would be opened officially together—even though the seven-county Oregon Coast Association headed by Albin W. Norblad pointed out that for the highway to be finished, five more bridges had to be built to replace ferry crossings.

One of the organization's main goals was to "Secure the most adequate ferry service possible over the unbridged rivers and bays along the highway, and to promote the replacement of these ferries with permanent bridges at the earliest possible date." The organization demanded that the bridges be built of wood, which would keep sawmills open and put more people back to work. To pay off the loan for their construction, the bridges would charge a toll to drivers.

Until the bridge's dedication the following spring, construction on it proceeded ahead of schedule. In fact, in a sense it opened even earlier than planned when in December of 1931, the ferry service at Gold Beach broke down, and cars and trucks backed up. "The ferry service was giving trouble and traffic had to be handled," said bridge engineer Marshall Dresser, "so we opened the bridge to limited traffic."

A few days later, the first and probably last marriage ceremony took place on the bridge. "After considerable debate," reported a local newspaper, "a decision was reached that since the groom had spent several month at work on the great $600,000 bridge, it would be most fitting to have the ceremony performed on the structure." So on a moonlit night at the center of the bridge, "Fern Wile, bridge worker, and Stella P. Terry of Salem were married at 8 o'clock."

But as spring drew near, a major slide occurred near the Cape Creek Bridge and Tunnel, which had been finished in March. Travelers were advised to use the old road above the tunnel. "Although [it is] very rough and muddy, [it] is passable," the Highway Commission announced. "As you may know from past experiences, this is a one-way road with steep grades and high centers."

Nevertheless, even during the dark times of the Depression, Gold Beach continued to meticulously plan the dedication of the new bridge from the opening ceremony to the final salute. When May 28, 1932 finally rolled around, people from all sections of the West Coast and from every walk of life attended. On that Saturday morning, the new bridge glistened in the early morning light. Boats lazily passed through its arches. And then music shattered the silence as a procession of bands from Seaside, Coos Bay,

Completed Rogue River Bridge, March 21, 1932

Coquille, Bandon, Crescent City, Roseburg, the American Legion, and the U.S. Coast Guard marched into view. Following the music was a mob of people noisily walking to the south side of the bridge. There they came to a barrier and stopped.

At the same time back in Washington D.C., President Herbert Hoover pushed a telegraph key from his oval office and sent a spark via Western Union across the continent to Coos Bay, and from there over the West Coast Telephone Company's lines to Gold Beach, where the spark dropped the barrier. The bridge was open, and the ceremonies began.

Four 4-H girls lifted a veil from a tablet that read: "Isaac Lee Patterson Memorial Bridge. Dedicated May 28, 1932 by the people of Oregon. In appreciation of his devotion to highway progress. Governor of Oregon, 1927-1930." Mrs. Isaac Lee Patterson, the governor's widow, then hung a wreath of Oregon grape over it.

Dignitaries spoke, bands played, the crowd sat down to a lunch of baked Chinook salmon, and Leslie M. Scott, chairman of the State Highway Commission, recounted the building of the road along Oregon's coast.

"Gradually, the projects in the various counties were extended," he said in his speech that day, "highway grades were surfaced, oiled and paved until today we have a finished highway 396 and one half miles in length."

And because a new bridge now provided one of the important last links on that great road, the Oregon Coast Highway from the California border to the Columbia River was finally open for business—if motorists could just endure the five remaining unbridged rivers and their slow-moving ferries.

Bridging Gaps
1933-1936

As 1933 began, Route 66 had already opened as the nation's great interstate highway, linking Chicago to Los Angeles; Congress had passed another gasoline tax to raise more money for roads; the speed limit in Oregon was 20 miles per hour in business districts and 45 miles per hour on the open road; arm signals were required of motorists when turning or stopping; and somebody needed to show the world that the five remaining ferries along Oregon Coast Highway were not significant obstacles to travel.

That spring, three men at the prompting of a local chamber of commerce took this job upon themselves: Tillamook mayor A.J. Swett, and chamber members John Schoroeder of Tillamook and

Building highway on north coast between Arch Cape and Hug Point, 1933

73

Gus Hafenbrach of Astoria. And so on a rainy Monday morning in early May, these three began the 420-mile drive from Astoria to Crescent City. Even though the rain continued all day, they made the trip in 8 hours and 40 minutes. Of their total time, they spent 47 minutes riding ferries and another 15 minutes changing a flat tire.

Yet they had made their journey before the height of the tourist season, and everyone knew that summer would once again bring with it long lines of frustrated drivers waiting for ferries. Even though the Oregon Coast Highway Association dropped its earlier demands that all bridges be built of wood, the problem remained: finding the money to build five bridges during the Depression, when banks were failing, jobs were scarce, and morale was low. One solution was to make the bridges pay for themselves by charging tolls: 20 cents for each automobile and driver, 5 cents for each additional passenger in the car, 5 cents for each passenger on a bus, and 60-90 cents per truck. "Bridges Virtually Certain To Be Toll," announced a *Siuslaw Oar* headline in June of 1933. But then the federal government stepped in.

With President Franklin Roosevelt's New Deal programs—such as the Civilian Conservation Corps (CCC) and the Public Works Administration (PWA)—helping to provide some of the jobs and lend some of the money for construction, the last watery gaps along the Oregon Coast Highway could be closed. Still, summer passed, the funding did not arrive, and many coast residents faced a long winter of unemployment.

"Organized relief will not be able to take care of the demands of the coming winter if work is not provided," the *Newport Journal* reported that September. "Our city, county and other relief agencies have about exhausted their means of providing for those who are out of work...People are beginning to talk and to believe that the Public Works program is merely political bunk."

By the end of September, however, the Northwest PWA office finally approved all five bridges. The only obstacle remaining was for Washington D.C. officials to accept the state's plan for repaying the construction debt: As bridges replaced ferries, use the money then going to the ferries to pay for the bridges.

"The cost of maintaining ferry service, if applied to payment of the bridge costs," reported the Highway Commission, "would pay for the bridges over the 30 year period." And if the payment were not met in that time, then both federal and state governments could charge a bridge toll to retire the remaining debt. But not everyone liked this last idea.

Charles H. Martin

"We must have free bridges along this great scenic highway to increase our tourist travel," said Oregon Governor Charles H. Martin, who was the sixth Oregon governor to hold office since the highway was approved in 1919.

Finally, in January of 1934 the Public Works Administration accepted the plan and approved financing of $5,102,620 for the construction of the last five bridges on the Oregon Coast Highway. Of this, the first $1,299,000 was to be a grant rather than a loan.

"This work," said the *Newport Journal*, "assures Newport and the entire coast of a badly needed payroll for the next two years."

Closing the last gaps in the Oregon Coast Highway was the job of Conde B. McCullough, bridge engineer for the Highway Commission since 1919. Over the next two years he had the responsibility of designing, supervising, and finishing the construction of the five major bridges that were to span, from north to south, Yaquina Bay at Newport, Alsea Bay at Waldport, the Siuslaw River at Florence, the Umpqua River at Reedsport, and Coos Bay at Coos Bay.

"McCullough rates the coast bridges as the most important of his career," said the *Coos Bay Times*, while McCullough him-

Alsea Bay Bridge at Waldport, Oregon

self called the project, "the biggest engineering job I ever super-
vised." He envisioned five magnificent bridges unique to their
individual settings, structures that would dazzle the world.

April of 1934 marked the beginning of the first of the five
bridges, the Alsea Bay Bridge at Waldport, to be built for an
estimated $685,000. Over the next two years, an average of
150 men worked for thirty hours each week for hourly wages
ranging from 50 cents for general laborers to $1.20 for skilled
workers. This was typical for all bridge construction during the
period, though the number of workers sometimes exceeded
two hundred.

"I went to work on the bridge...wheeling cement until
1936," recalled one worker. "They had walkways built out to
where they was pouring cement, big ramps. They had a cement plant set up there at the end of the bridge that didn't shut

Yaquina Bay Bridge at Newport, Oregon, January 22, 1936

down. It ran 24 hours a day. It stormed, but they poured cement anyway. Sometimes it was so foggy that from the cement mixer you couldn't see out to where you were going to pour."

By the fall of 1936, all five bridges with their soaring spires and elegant arches, their long viaducts and wide roadways and sidewalks were finished. The result was a marvel of engineering.

"The bridge has a total length of 3,260 feet with a 27 foot

Yaquina Bay Bridge at Newport, Oregon under construction, March 10, 1936

Yaquina Bay Bridge at Newport, Oregon finished, September 6, 1936

roadbed, and a three and a half foot sidewalk on each side," the *Newport Journal* said of the Yaquina Bay Bridge, though all five bridges were similarly impressive in their size and scope. "The north approach rests upon a solid bluff practically 100 feet above the bay, then comes a 350 foot steel span which reaches to the edge of the channel, a 600 foot steel arch, the top of which reaches 245 feet above the water, crosses the main channel with 138 feet between the bottom of the deck and the water. Next comes another 350 foot steel span and then five concrete arches, the longest one 265 feet. A 550 foot concrete viaduct forms the south approach."

At dedication ceremonies along the coast, thousands of people celebrated the final links to the Coast Highway and the outside world. Long parades, loud bands, big crowds, and inspiring speeches marked each occasion. "Of the six bridges on the Oregon Coast none in my opinion excels the Coos Bay Bridge in beauty of design," Oregon Governor Martin said in his speech at the dedication of the bridge, though his remarks were also a tribute to Conde B. McCullough and his concrete creations. "More than a mile in length with its great steel cantilever truss, elevated 150 feet above the main channel and

Coos Bay Bridge construction, November 27, 1934

Coos Bay Bridge, July 26, 1935

Coos Bay Bridge, August 2, 1935

Coos Bay Bridge, August 6, 1935

Coos Bay Bridge, September 20, 1935

Coos Bay Bridge, September 25, 1935

Coos Bay Bridge, October 30, 1935

Coos Bay bridge December 4, 1935

Diver at Coos Bay Bridge construction, with enlarged inset, June 18, 1936

Coos Bay Bridge, finished, July 7, 1936

with a central span of 793 feet, the construction of this bridge is an engineering triumph, a symbol of human genius, courage and effort."

Such an achievement, of course, came with a high price tag. Leslie M. Scott, former Highway Commissioner, estimated the total cost of building the Oregon Coast Highway was "$25 million of which $6 million has been used in constructing the five bridges."

Yet no matter what the cost, these amazing bridges provided the final link in the wonder that was the Oregon Coast Highway.

"If we engineers had souls, which I doubt, we might have to take to the back roads to keep from blushing every time we see some of the things we have done," Conde B. McCullough once wrote. "But on the other hand, I'm kinda human like the rest of humanity, and I'll admit that there's at least two bridges I've had a hand in, and when I look at them, I kinda figure I'll have some alibi when I see St. Peter. Not all of 'em, you understand, but some of 'em did come out so good they make life worth living."

Siuslaw River Bridge at Florence, Oregon, April 4, 1935

Siuslaw River Bridge at Florence, Oregon, April 19, 1935

Siuslaw River Bridge at Florence, Oregon, July 6, 1935

Siuslaw River Bridge and ferry at Florence, Oregon, November 30, 1935

Siuslaw River Bridge at Florence, Oregon, December 17, 1935

Siuslaw River Bridge at Florence, Oregon, February 14, 1936

Siuslaw River Bridge at Florence, Oregon, Finished, February 21, 1936

Umpqua River Bridge at Reedsport, Oregon, October 8, 1935

Umpqua River Bridge at Reedsport, Oregon, October, 1935

Umpqua River Bridge at Reedsport, Oregon, October18, 1935

91

Umpqua River Bridge at Reedsport, Oregon, Finished, April 7, 1936

In 1919 Benjamin F. Jones had envisioned a road that would help free the coast from its isolation, a road that would help industry, generate tourism, and provide jobs and access to residents and visitors alike. Even though he didn't live to see that dream become a reality, Mr. Jones can rest easy—in 1936, seventeen years after its beginning in the Oregon State Legislature, the Roosevelt Highway was at last finished.

Like a silver thread I wind my
Way,
Through forests, vales and hills:
By sparkling brooks of water clear;
O'er mountain grades and fills...
My course is laid through grandest
Views
Of mountain crest and valley
Stream.
Where sweetest native flowers
Bloom,
And scenic beauty rules supreme.
—Author unknown
Tribute to the Roosevelt Highway
c. 1936

Benjamin F. Jones
1857-1925

Index

A

B

C

K

L

M

N

O

About the Author

A t San Diego State College, the only class in which Joe Blakely claims he excelled was the writing of history. After graduating with a liberal arts degree, he explored numerous job opportunities, first in real estate sales, then in work as a real estate appraiser, at both the government level and later for a Federal savings and loan. After a number of years in real estate, Joe bought and operated a second hand store. Later, he found a position as a public safety officer for the University of Oregon, from which position he retired in 1999.

Joe Blakely
with wife Saundra Miles

photo by Pauline Rughani

After retirement from full-time work, Joe felt he already had good exercise habits, but needed to keep his brain functioning, so he decided to return to his early love of history and began writing about the history of Oregon, supplementing his writings with photographs, in historical photo-journalism. His first subject was an old dilapidated building on the bay of Bandon, on the southern Oregon coast. He wrote an article supplemented with photographs, and to his utter amazement, the editor of the Oregon Historical Quarterly Magazine published "The Nestle Condensary in Bandon" in winter of 2003.

Since then, Joe has written seven books: *The Bellfountain Giant Killers*, the story of a small Oregon high school that won the 1937 state basketball championship; *The Tall Firs*, an account of the University of Oregon winning the first NCAA basketball championship in 1939; this book, *Lifting Oregon Out of The Mud: Building the Oregon Coast Highway; A Tribute to McArthur*

Court, the University of Oregon's basketball pavilion built in 1926-27; and *Eugene's Civic Stadium: From Muddy Football Games to Professional Baseball.*

Mr. Blakely also extracted information from these historical works to write two novels: *The Heirloom,* a novel that takes place in Bandon, Oregon in 1921, and *Kidnapped, on Oregon's Coast Highway (1926).*

Joe is currently working on a novel about a team of baseball rejects, and their threatened stadium.

Lifting Oregon Out of The Mud is being republished for many reasons. One reason is the fortuitous discovery of some photographs taken in Tillamook County in the early 1920s from the family collection of Lorraine Eckhardt, who was kind enough to share her photographs with him. These early photographs are a poignant reminder of the tremendous effort it took to build the Oregon Coast Highway.

Lastly, he credits his writing success to Mark Highberger, publisher and editor of Bear Creek Press, and to Dan and Barbara Gleason of CraneDance Publications.

For autographed copies of any of his books, contact Joe Blakely at 541-688-4643, or write to P.O. Box 51561, Eugene, Oregon 97405.